The C Word

Poetry collection

NAOMI FLAHERTY

The C Word - Poetry Collection
Naomi Flaherty © 2023

First Published by Compass-Publishing UK
ISBN 978-1-915962-18-8

Typeset by The Book Refinery Ltd
www.TheBookRefinery.com

Disclaimer
Please note this book references some difficult themes and subject
matter that may be triggering or difficult for individuals to read.

For all those affected by the 'C' word.
You are not alone.

Contents

Introduction

In my line of work, the 'C' word has a whole different meaning to the one that faced me back in September 2022.

You hear the word 'cancer', often thrown around, on the TV, cancer charities and people raising money to combat it. Often hearing about other people having it but what you don't expect to hear is that you have it. You also don't anticipate how much that little 'C' word can alter your life and the impact it has on those around you.

The 'C' word...having it, came as a shock, however my first thoughts after getting my head around it, were about being positive and approaching the disease with strength and conviction in that I would beat it. Overall, I feel I maintained this but don't get me wrong, there were bad days, days I did not know what to do with myself and days that were beyond hard and days where I needed those around me to have the same positivity.

I started writing in a mindful journal, given to me by my Mother-in-Law, whilst having treatment and this helped me process what was happening to me, write down my frustrations when I felt unheard and note positive quotes to look at.

Writing poems randomly came about when I was nearing the end of treatment and I would write about my experiences of having and more importantly, surviving cancer as a way of reflecting on what I had endured. For me, having cancer did not really hit home until after I had beaten it.

I decided that I wanted to share those experiences I had written about with others. Most importantly for me, I wanted to share them with the intention to hopefully help others that may be going through similar experiences to mine.

These poems are obviously personal to me, but I hope they may resonate with others and help them understand things about their own treatment, acknowledge their fears and bad days; knowing it's ok, not to be ok, (something a friend of mine used to tell me all the time, which really helped), and even help answer questions about their cancer journey that no-one else will really understand and highlight the importance of a having a good support network around you – no matter what that looks like.

I hope my story serves as a reminder that this journey is tough enough, you need to be accepting of help from those around you that are willing to offer it, (something I initially found hard).

Additionally, I wanted my poems, to highlight and raise awareness of Lymphoma. Lymphoma is the most common blood cancer in the UK, but I had never heard of it until it affected me, as so often is the case. More awareness means catching this horrible disease early, meaning more people can fight it and win.

Finally, it has always been my dream to write a book. Ironic that something like the 'C' word, which wanted to take my life from me has given me the inspiration to make a dream come true and give my life further meaning. My little way of telling cancer to...well you know...the 'F' word off...

As I now tell my husband, it'll take more than that to get rid of me.

I want my daughter to be proud of me and know how much she was my daily inspiration to get better, to carry on when it got tough, to fight and to win.

My Story

Back in May 2022 after a very normal shower, whilst washing my hair, I found a lump on the left side of my neck. I didn't think much of it at the time but after a quick Google search, I decided to make a doctor's appointment for a week's time, as I would have had it 2 weeks by then and figured I'd just cancel the appointment if I needed to.

I went to the doctors and was told to wait 2 more weeks. In that time, I found a pea sized lump on the right side of my neck. I made another appointment and was told I'd have an ultrasound. The ultrasound happened two months later and all I remember from it was the radiologist saying that it didn't look right but he couldn't say anymore. I remember feeling at the time that I did not have a good feeling about this but ever the optimist, I just tried to stay positive and think the same way. I did not anticipate it would be anything too serious.

I had a second ultrasound in July 2022. Again, the same radiologist told me that what he saw did not look normal and he was seeing things he should not be seeing. Even at this point I was not thinking it would be anything serious. I was also given a Laryngoscopy, (where a small tube goes into your nose and down your throat), not pleasant but over with quickly. I then had a chest X-Ray. Then it was a waiting game. I enjoyed the summer holidays and went back to work in September.

On 15th September 2022, I received a devastating phone call whilst at work from a doctor, to tell me that I had Lymphoma. To say I was shocked would be an understatement. At 32 I never expected to hear the word cancer. I also never expected to hear that kind of news over the phone, from a doctor I had never met or spoken to before.

I walked out of the classroom I had been sitting in to take the call, walked into my head teacher's office and I remember her asking "What did they say? What's wrong?" and I burst into tears. I stood in her embrace, for how long I cannot remember, and I could not stop crying. When I finally did, we sat in her office and talked. She asked me if I wanted to go home but I really didn't. I carried on working and getting things done, knowing I was then off until the following Tuesday.

At first, I needed time to process the news and I kept it to myself, telling my husband the next day and close family and friends after a couple of weeks. It was a very difficult time, not knowing at that point which type of Lymphoma I had, what stage I was and what was going to happen next. I did receive a prompt appointment with Oncology/Haematology the day after I received my diagnosis.

I had to wait a week and a half to see my consultant who told me I had Hodgkin Lymphoma (HL). Having done my own research I felt quite relieved that it wasn't Non-Hodgkin Lymphoma. HL is more easily treated but aggressive.

We talked through everything, and I had my PET/CT scan the same day. It was a lot to take in and I know at times I wasn't taking it in, but my husband was there to support me, and we briefly touched on the treatment I would be receiving. This was the first time I had heard the word chemotherapy and to me, my oncologist may as well have been talking about someone else because it had not hit me still that I had cancer and that this was happening to me.

The scan revealed I had stage 3 HL - the Lymphoma was in my neck, chest and spleen. I had large masses on my chest and my consultant was quite surprised that I'd had no other symptoms other than the lumps on my neck.

Given the large masses and being stage 3, there was a degree of urgency to get started with my treatment. There was a slight problem...one of my wisdom teeth had become infected and I needed to have it removed, on closer inspection and a couple of X-rays later, it was determined that all four of my wisdom teeth needed to be removed. My consultant advised it would be better to remove them all and then start chemotherapy, so they didn't cause me problems later. I had them all removed under local anaesthetic on 14th October 2022.

At another appointment with my consultant, it was discussed that I would need to have two intensive cycles of treatment – escalated BEACOPP. BEACOPP is named after the drugs used:

B – bleomycin

E – etoposide

A – doxorubicin (also called Adriamycin®)

C – cyclophosphamide

O – vincristine (also called Oncovin®)

P – procarbazine

P – prednisolone, a steroid.

Each cycle of BEACOPP would take three weeks. Then I'd have another PET/CT scan to see how things were going. I was told about symptoms to expect from treatment, to name a few...

- Potential allergic reaction to any of the chemo drugs.
- Any of the chemo drugs leaking outside the vein.
- Infections due to decreasing white blood cells.
- Anaemia
- Bruising and bleeding
- Nausea and Sickness
- Sore/dry mouth, throat and ulcers
- Constipation as well as diarrhoea
- Change in appetite – wanting to eat more and not wanting to eat much at all.
- Irritated bladder/pink urine caused by the chemo drug, Doxorubicin.
- Muscle and joint pain, including jaw pain.
- Peripheral Neuropathy (numb or tingling sensation in the hands and feet).
- Skin and nail changes

- Effects on the heart – tight chest and changes to your heartbeat.
- High blood sugar
- Hair loss

There are others but I won't bore you with those. What symptoms did you have? I hear you ask...might be easier to tell you which ones I did not have...I did not have any allergic reactions and I did not have chemo leaking out of my veins and no bleeding but the rest, yes, I had them all.

I remember feeling very overwhelmed on my first day of treatment – 19th October 2022, (yes, just five days after having my wisdom teeth removed). I had a Peripherally Inserted Central Catheter (PICC) line, (used to deliver the chemo drugs), inserted in the morning and around 7 hours of treatment. A very long, emotional and arduous day. It was very surreal at first and then it really hit home for me that I was having chemotherapy and I had cancer. It had been easy not to think too much about it until then.

I had a whole bag of medications I had been given and, in all honesty, I had no clue about them. A nurse sat with me on that first day and talked me through the meds; doses, when to take them and possible side effects. I absorbed very little of that information. Given that my husband had not been allowed to stay with me in the Haematology Day unit, I felt like I was doing it all alone and I could not retain the information. I am really lucky that a member of my family used to be a brilliant nurse, so I sent her pictures of my meds, and she sent me a detailed list of all of them with descriptions that I was then able to save on a note on my phone and refer to.

The next day was awful too. I had not registered that I needed to take anti-sickness tablets prior to my chemo being administered, (it was the only tablets I had not looked at in my big bag), so when the nurses asked me if I had taken my Metoclopramide, I had no clue what they were talking about and they assumed I had taken it. During my last treatment of the day, I began to be violently sick, to the point I could not then drive myself home and had to be collected by my sister-in-law, who then had to pull over three times on the way home so I could puke on the road side...I then proceeded to be sick every 15-20 minutes for about 4 hours and then every hour for a further 5 hours until it eased off. Suffice to say, I did not forget to take my anti-sickness meds again.

After around 15 days from beginning treatment, I was quite poorly and spent a few days in bed. It was at this point my hair began falling out in clumps. I remember getting out of bed on the third day of feeling ill and pulling my hairband out and lots of hair going with it. My hair was matted and the more I brushed my hair, the more came out. I was quite shocked as I had not expected it to come out as quickly as that and I could not believe the mass of hair that had accumulated on the floor or my bathroom.

One of the hardest things for me about treatment was the side effect of losing my hair. I had blonde hair I could almost sit on and had had long hair for as long as I could remember. I quite honestly found it traumatic, and I couldn't even talk about it or discuss what and how it would happen, until it started to happen. I did ignore it and I buried my head in the sand about it, so I decided I wanted to turn it into a positive and I, along with my amazing family, friends and work colleagues raised over £1,000 for Lymphoma Action and I 'braved the shave'. A lovely friend of mine who is a hairdresser cut my hair as best as she could, and my husband shaved the rest of for me after a few days. I remember feeling quite empowered by this but at the same time it took a long time to be comfortable without any hair. I didn't look like me anymore and now actually looked like a sick person. Something I did not relish.

Making the decision to cut and shave my hair and doing it for a good cause gave me back some element of control. Throughout this process you really feel as if all the control has been taken away and it is important to find something, anything, that can give you back some power.

It wasn't plain sailing and I had to have a platelet transfusion on 1st November 2022 and unfortunately due to an infection from my wisdom tooth extraction, I later developed sepsis.

I was admitted into resus on 18th November 2022. I very nearly died and had everyone very worried about me. I had woken up on the day not feeling well at all with a temperature. I was home with my then 2-year-old daughter and my husband at work. I managed to get down the stairs, (shuffling on my bum, one step at a time, while my daughter held my hand). I text my husband to come home and he found me laid on the kitchen floor. He took me straight to hospital where I remained for 8 days. I had Neutropenic Sepsis. The infection had developed from my tooth extraction. My face was terribly swollen, I was in a lot of pain, cold, clammy, shivering, high temperature and tachycardic. I was being asked by the doctors' if I agreed to CPR and if I was ok with them 'jumping on my chest' if they needed to. I obviously said yes but had no real comprehension of how serious things were at that time. It did not register until a few days later when my consultant explained that I could have died.

A hard lesson learnt about making sure to call my emergency number in the future if I felt ill. I was given copious amounts of antibiotics, a blood transfusion, a platelet transfusion and lots of supplements. At one point my blood pressure bottomed out and that was also a scary time and took hours to get it back to normal. I moved around the hospital a bit, having a room on my own for a few days and was then moved onto the Haematology ward. I met some lovely ladies whilst there and they helped me battle feelings of being overwhelmed by the experience.

I had low blood pressure, kept feeling dizzy and fell in the toilet one morning, bashing my head on the door as I went down. I had blacked out for a few seconds so this had led to an MRI and an extra day stay in the hospital. All I can say is the staff on that ward were amazing! I was really looked after there.

I was eventually able to leave hospital after 8 long days, just in time for my daughter's 3rd birthday party, which was just the best feeling ever!

For a time, things improved and on 2nd December 2022, after my 2nd PET/CT scan, I found out I was in complete remission! I cannot tell you what a relief that was. I was quite shocked for this to happen so soon but unbelievably ecstatic. This meant my treatment was de-escalated and I started receiving ABVD (-the B) chemotherapy treatment.

ABVD is named after the initials of the chemotherapy drugs used in the treatment.

A – doxorubicin (Adriamycin®)

B – bleomycin

V – vinblastine (Velbe®)

D – dacarbazine (DTIC).

Unfortunately, on 13th December, I ended up in hospital with sepsis again...just a 4 day stay this time. I had contracted...the Flu...I was isolated within the Haematology ward this time and was struggling with dizziness. At this point I'd lost 3.2kg's in weight, another side effect. I had low energy, loss of appetite, muscle aches and a sore, dry mouth. I felt quite lonely during this period, however again, the staff on the Haematology ward were great, checking on me regularly, stopping by for a chat and doing everything they could to make my stay as comfortable as possible.

Another blood transfusion on 24th December 2022. Then I started my 4th cycle on 3rd January 2023. I am proud to say that I had continued to work throughout this period.

My last two cycles of treatment were the worst and on 31st January 2023, I stopped working as much. Up to this point, from October, I'd been working from home. Fatigue and muscle aches had really set in, but I was so close to the finish line. I counted down every week, every treatment, every day, every hour...every minute of my beeping chemo machine when receiving treatment.

The next couple of months were gruelling but I was extremely lucky to have such an amazing network of support around me.

I cannot thank my husband enough for all his unwavering support throughout and my daughter, she often kept me going, (without realising), and doing things when I really didn't want to. Some days it was a struggle to get out of bed, but I had to, for them.

My Mum, brother, sister, in laws, friends and colleagues were incredible. Even just letting me know I was in their thoughts really helped me get through the tough days, getting advice and having conversations that were nothing to do with cancer. Everyone around me had maintained such a high level of positivity and it really made all the difference.

I finished chemotherapy treatment - my 6th cycle in total, 16 treatments, on 14th March 2023. Just 13 days after my 33rd birthday. I'm extremely pleased to say I'm still in remission!

I now have a different perspective on life. I think it would be hard not to after facing the 'C' word. If I want to go on a holiday, I am going. If I want to try something new, I am doing it. If I feel a certain way, you'll know about it, and I don't take anything for granted anymore.

I take each day as it comes and I'm living my best life.

It's going to take more than cancer to bring me down!

The Lump

It's hair wash day today. My least favourite day...
When your hair is as long as mine, you'd understand why...
What is that? Nothing, I'm sure. I get out the shower and get dry.
I feel it again...a lump...on my neck.

I think little of it and a week passes by.
The lump...it's still there.
I do some 'Googling' and make a doctor's appointment. It could
be cancer but that seems rare.
Possibly an infection but I feel fine.
I don't have any other symptoms so that's a good sign.

Two weeks to the day since I found the lump and I see the
doctor who tells me to wait.
More lumps I find on my neck, these are small.
It's time to make another call.
Back to the doctors I go.
They tell me, 'Please don't worry, we'll get you in for an

ultrasound scan'.
Follow the system, follow the plan.
There's nothing else I can do now but wait and see.
Easy for them to say but I agree.

It's been two months since I found the lump. I have the scan.
Something doesn't look right. That's all that is said.
Bad thoughts emanate in my head.
A biopsy is now needed.

It's been three months since I found the lump and its biopsy time.
All I can hope is that everything is fine.
About 6 weeks I will have to wait.
Not too long to find out my fate.

Diagnosed

A phone call, a distant voice, the c word lingers in the air.

No thoughts, some thoughts...one thought. It's not fair!

I sit in an empty classroom where I received the news.

Anger tears through me momentarily like a lit fuse.

What was said? I can't remember. I made notes but they make little sense now.

I'll need to tell my family, my friends but how?

All of that will have to wait, I need to get back to work, back to the office I go.

My boss asks, 'What's wrong? What did they say?'. The tears start to flow.

Uncontrolled shaking takes over my body, I cannot breathe, this is not real.

A long embrace, a snotty shoulder to cry on literally...I cannot feel.

To go or stay, that is the question. I choose to stay and focus my thoughts before I drive home.

One thing I know, I can't do this alone.

At least now I know. I have been diagnosed.

I have cancer. Lymphoma.

Lymph what?

Lymphoma. 'I'm sorry to tell you that you have Lymphoma Naomi'.
I didn't catch the doctors name or what hospital he was calling from.
This man does not even know me.

Lymphoma...that's what the doctor said.
'Do you know what that is?' He speaks.
Thoughts twist and turn in my head.
I think I do...A 'blood cancer' he speaks. It affects the blood in different ways.

'You'll get a call from Haematology soon'.
He speaks again, this doctor I don't know.
A static builds in my head like an annoying tune.
That's it, conversation over, he must go.

Lymphoma. I have it or so I'm told.
I don't know much so Google it is.
This one little word has made me age in a day, and I feel old.
I keep it to myself for the day so my husband can have his.

Lymphoma. There are two types as I read.
Hodgkin and Non-Hodgkin.
Both seem bad but non-Hodgkin takes the lead.

The 'C word' plan and scan

I meet with my consultant early on a Tuesday morning.
My husband goes with me for support.
Lots of things are said, some I don't remember but it's all very informing.

I'm having a PET-CT scan as well this morning.
I must have an injection - a radiotracer.
It will show where my cancer is forming.

I don't have long to wait for the PET-CT scan results, only a day!
I'm nervous but I want to know.
Off to the hospital to see what my consultant has to say.

My consultant explains my cancer treatment.
The treatment is going to be intensive to begin with.
I have large masses on my chest, and it could spread quickly so we're in agreement.

Hodgkin's Lymphoma is apparently easy to treat but is an
aggressive cancer.
I have it in my neck, chest and spleen so it's stage three.
Chemotherapy is the only answer.

I will do chemo on days 1, 2, 3, 8 and 15 and this will be a cycle
in total beginning in October.
I will have 6 cycles over 6 months.
No alcohol for me, it's time to become a teetotaller and stay
sober.

I'll need a PICC line fitted as this is the safest way to have
chemo.
This will be done on day one of treatment.
I'll go to the unit in Haemo.

I've also got to have all my wisdom teeth out.
Not looking forward to that.
I'm having a local, so I'll be awake throughout.

It's starting to feel a bit more real now as things are progressing.
I'm going to enjoy every moment before I start my treatment.
And try not to keep stressing.

'Chemo Day'

The day came for me to begin chemo and have my PICC line inserted.
Nervous, fearful, anxious, worried, overwhelmed, lonely and sad.
Only some of the emotions I felt that could not be averted.
This was just the beginning of my journey; I'd be getting better so in part I was glad.

I was assigned a coloured chair...blue, very apt for the situation.
I sat alone as my husband was told he couldn't accompany me.
A bag of pills was placed in front of me and so began my education.
I felt so overwhelmed and lonely I just wanted to flee.

Nurses talking at me like all this was normal.
I sat in my blue chair alone, the reality of receiving treatment sinking in.
My nurse not so friendly but formal.
I start to cry without anyone even noticing...a small win.

I had read my treatment would be an hour and hadn't been told
any different until I asked.
Little did I know that it was going to be six!
The tears began to flow again but were quickly masked.
Chemo...not a quick fix.

The magnitude of what I was embarking on had just hit me like
Tyson Fury did Wilder...the third time I mean.
Just like that fight, this one was not going to be won after one
round.
I felt insignificant, lost and unseen.
Sat in the day unit, chemo running through me, waiting for my
machine to beep - this would become a familiar sound.

I had arrived at the hospital at 9am and got home at 7pm
absolutely shattered.
I tried to look through my endless tablets given that I'd
absorbed very little that was said to me, but I could not.
Emotional, my brain scattered.
I went upstairs, the tears fell again as I stared in the mirror,
thinking this...is a lot.

I slept very little that night and woke to start the process all
over again.
Feeling slightly more prepared than the day before.
A pink chair this time...it's time to begin...count to ten.
Nauseous, I start to feel sick but try to ignore.

Bleomycin, Etoposide, Doxorubicin (also called Adriamycin),
Cyclophosphamide, Vincristine (also called Oncovin),
Procarbazine. Oh, and Prednisolone (a steroid).
This is my chemo regime so many names to remember.
So many cells will be destroyed.
This will be the case until November.

I'm lucky I have a family member who used to be a nurse, she
helped me a lot.
So knowledgeable, she explained all the medication.
If she hadn't gone through it all with me, I'd have surely forgot.
So much to remember, names, side effects and information.

I come to the end of day 2 and the nausea becomes more. I'm
sick. I'm collected from hospital because I can't drive.
I continue to be sick, again and again until there's nothing left
but still it comes.
I need help, I need my husband and wait for him to arrive.
Finally, the sickness succumbs.

Day 3 and I feel like a pro,
This cancer, it can just go.

Hair today...gone tomorrow

Long, blonde hair. This is what people see when they look at me.
Hair I could almost sit on to a degree.

I loved my hair, apart from when it was time to wash...
It would take so long, oh my gosh.

Now I'd give anything for it to take so long.
I really miss my hair now that it is gone.

I remember being told I would lose my hair.
I had no idea how much I would care.

More than the doctors and nurses anyway...
More than they could comprehend any day.

It started to fall out on 2nd November 2022.
Such a traumatic thing to go through.

It probably sounds stupid.
To be so attached to something rooted.

It came out in clumps, all on that day.
I remember it so clearly even today.
My friend cut the hair and I cried as she did.
I couldn't stand it, I wanted rid.

I got home and couldn't let my daughter see.
I wasn't ready for her to look at the new me.
For a couple of days, I hid it with a hat.
In front of the mirror, I sat.

I didn't recognise the person staring back at me.
I needed it all gone. I wanted to feel free.

My husband got the clippers and shaved the rest for me.
At first, I didn't want to see.

Then I felt sort of liberated.
Kind of invigorated...

I didn't want to look sick with a bald head.
But better that than be dead.

My daughter wanted to see my 'hair'...I had to submit...
'Where's your hair gone Mummy? I don't like it'.

Out of the mouths of babes. I told her, 'It'll grow back soon,
don't worry'.
Secretly hoping it would in fact hurry.

In that moment I think I reassured myself that it would turn
out right.
And that this was just another part of my fight.

Long, blonde hair. This is what people saw when they looked at me.

I mourned the loss of my long, blonde hair.
No longer feeling such despair.
Now it does not define me. There is more to me than you can see.

Fatigue, Fatigue, Fatigue

Can't move, don't want to.
So little energy.
What is this lethargy?

Fatigue, fatigue, fatigue

Can't move, don't want to.
So so tired.
Why is so much effort required?

Fatigue, fatigue, fatigue

Can't move, don't want to.
So weakened I feel.
How do I conceal?

Fatigue, fatigue, fatigue

Can't move, don't want to.
I've done nothing but feel exhausted.
Why were these symptoms never reported?

Fatigue, fatigue, fatigue

Can't move, don't want to.
So emotionally, physically and mentally draining.
What can I do to keep from complaining?

Fatigue, fatigue, fatigue

Can't move, don't want to.
So debilitating, my husband must do everything for me.
How grateful I am, I hope he can see?

Fatigue, fatigue, fatigue

Can't move, don't want to.
So many muscle aches.
How much more can I take?

Fatigue, fatigue, fatigue

Can't move, have to.
So close now, I'm nearly there.
How do I get up out of this chair?

Fatigue, fatigue, fatigue

Can't move, have to.
So, get up and get on.
This feeling will soon be gone.

Pictures from left to right

My hair before chemo

After my tooth extraction – 14/10/22

My first day of chemo – 19/10/22

Braving the shave with my husband – 05/11/22

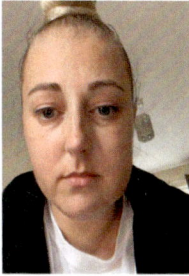

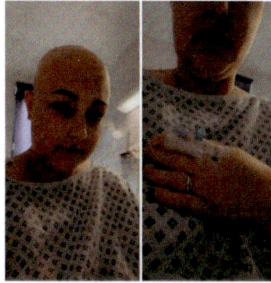

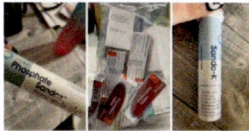

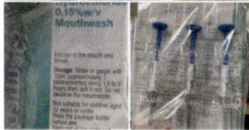

Many headscarves and wigs...

In hospital with sepsis – Nov 22

My amazing wig my sister-in-law took me to get, (priceless and only possible with help from my family) – Dec 22

Medications

My hair journey.

Getting out of hospital for my daughter's 3rd birthday party – 26/11/22

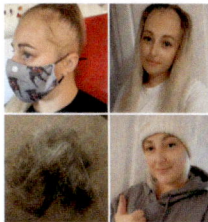

Pictures from left to right

Support network – my amazing family.

Fur babies

Last chemo – 14/03/23

PICC line removed – 21/03/23

3 months prior to treatment and 3 months post treatment – Aug 22/June 23

My amazing support network – Together with friends, family and work colleagues, we raised £1,035 for Lymphoma Action.

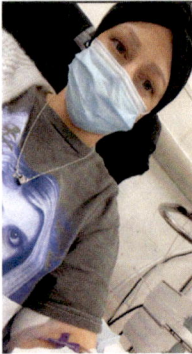

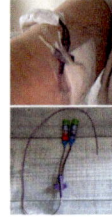

103%

£1,035
raised of **£1,000** target
by **33 supporters**

In my chemo bag I pack...

In my chemo bag I pack...
A hat, it's black.

In my chemo bag I pack...
Some biscuits for a snack.

In my chemo bag I pack...
In case it rains, a Mack.

In my chemo bag I pack...
My well-being journal to note my thoughts down.
Attempting a smile from a frown.

In my chemo bag I pack...
A good book to read.
My mind I hope it will feed.

In my chemo bag I pack...
My air pods, an early Christmas present from the hubby.
I'm so very lucky.

In my chemo bag I pack...
A Disney colouring book and pens from a friend.
Colouring Mickey and Minnie until treatment end.

In my chemo bag I pack...
A face mask.
Wearing these through treatment is no easy task.

Serious Sepsis

I don't feel well this morning,
In fact, I feel appalling.
So nauseous and dizzy, this is galling.

My daughter woke up which got me out of bed,
Now she's needs to be fed.

I'm not quite ready to go downstairs yet,
I won't worry my husband, don't want him to fret.

I lay in bed for a bit longer and put the TV on.
Hopefully this feeling will soon be gone.

A couple of hours pass by and my daughter's getting hungry,
she can't wait.
Why am I in such a state?

I'm struggling even standing.
Walking down the stairs will be demanding.

I sit on my bum to go down the stairs one at a time.
My daughter holds my hand, one step at a time.

We get to the bottom, and I cannot get up at all.
I can't risk it, what if I fall?

I crawl to the kitchen and feel so dizzy even on my knees.
I don't feel as sick, it's starting to ease.

Now I feel cold and clammy, my heart is racing.
What now? What else could I be facing?

I start to shiver, and I have a chill,
I must go on; I have the will.

I fall twice and briefly pass out.
My nurse has arrived to do my bloods, she knocks on the door,
but I can't even shout.

I managed to send off a text to my husband, but I don't know
how.
"I need you to come home... now!".

I lie on the kitchen floor,
My daughter lies next to me and then goes to the door.

My husband is here and so is the nurse,
He tries hard not to curse.

They get me up and off to hospital I go.
What is wrong with me? I need to know.

I'm seen in A+E quickly.
I must look sickly.

The nurse tells me I have Neutropenic Sepsis...I'm tachycardic
too.
It presents a bit like the flu.

Off to resus I go...
Everything goes slow.
Talks of doing CPR...
The Sepsis has gone quite far.

Antibiotics, lots of fluids, cannulas and transfusions.
Doctors, nurses, HCA's, cleaners, plenty of intrusions.

8 days later and finally I could leave.
Just in time to attend my daughter's third birthday party and
time for a reprieve.

I'm not a believer in God, but I thank him all the same.
To acknowledge something, you don't believe in may seem
lame...

All I can say is there's something about nearly dying,
That makes you feel alive and want to keep trying.

Chemo Fog

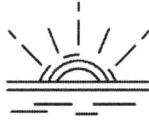

I'm in a daydream, what's that?
Someone's talking to me...
I can't even follow the chat.
The fog has me, will I ever be free?

All I can think of is how tired I am.
I'm struggling to remember things,
And have a short concentration span.
What else can cancer bring?

It can be hard to think clearly,
What was I going to say in reply?
I almost had it on the tip of my tongue, nearly.
So frustrated, I sigh.

Normally I'm the organised one,
Almost prepared with a plan.
There's the thought, there it is, oh it's gone.
I want to remember, I will remember, I can.

Everyday tasks must be done one at a time.
Too much can be overwhelming now.
Listen to me whine...
My doctor says the veil will lift but how?

Anyway, where was I?
I'm back to work and doing my thing.
I'm so determined to succeed and fly high.
The fog is slowly lifting, it's not as dark in here, a light is
turning on, ding.

Remission

There is something on your chest she says.
The thoughts spin round my head as I imagine more chemo,
treatment, suffering in all new ways.
It's nothing serious she explains, just some scar tissue from the
treatment.
My unshed tears recede like my hairline, a deep breathe in and
a long breath out.
"You're in remission", she says. I want to shout!
Yes!

"You're in remission". Remission...remission. The words echo in
my mind.
I honestly cannot believe it! I think I'm in shock. I never
expected this so soon. How has this happened already? I'm so
pleased there was nothing else to find!
Why am I questioning this? This is amazing, brilliant,
wonderful, remarkable.
She's still speaking...I need to listen to what else she has to say.
All I can think, is what an amazing day!

They're going to keep an eye on me, but it all looks good.
I'll still have to go to the hospital for them to take blood.
Treatment must continue too...I have got to have the full 6 cycles.
I know I should be happy, I'm in remission after all.
But that chemo...it's no ball.

I feel so bad for thinking this way,
I need to keep those thoughts at bay.
I can do this. I will see it through to the finish.
I've kicked cancer's butt so far to be in complete remission.
I have won this fight and I will win this battle, my positivity
coming to fruition.

The flu!

My face...it looks different...swollen somehow...
My hands too, my fingers, oh wow.
My heart is beating faster and faster.
My breathing is more difficult now and I'm breathless.
To be honest, I feel like a feverish mess.

My breathing is rapid, shallow and I breathe fast.
Maybe I should give it some time, until this has passed?
No, I can't wait, not this time.
It feels so familiar these symptoms I have again...
I'm feeling confused, I have a fever, I'm in pain.

Back to hospital on the Haematology ward.
To resus and on the unit to be stored.
It's Sepsis again...but how?
Some tests later and I find out I've got...the flu!
Into isolation you go...shoo!

Just in hospital for a four day stay.
They might want to keep me longer, hopefully the doctors
won't get their way.
I thought cancer was bad but sepsis ... not so great either,
especially for the second time.
Now I know what to look for, even with the flu.
I know the signs and symptoms; I know what to do.

Never ending chemo

Despite being in remission, more chemo is needed.
Got to finish the cycles, make sure the cancer has receded.

It seems harder now to endure,
Just got to make sure it's gone for sure.

It feels like it's getting harder each time I go.
Treatment day is so slow!

Almost there now, got to go with the flow.
Just a few more cycles to go.

The last two are the hardest I have known to date.
I do not feel great.

So close to the finish line now,
I feel like I should take a bow.

It has been a long slog,
From muscle aches to the chemo fog.

I did it! I am still here!
Through the ups and the downs, clarity and fear.

I did it! I am still here!
The last day of chemo let's all cheer!

My reasons to live

I look at my little mini me,
with her big, beautiful blue eyes staring back at me.
Will she ever know how much she means to me?
My little 'Baby T'.
She's keeps me going on days that are so hard.
My Baby T, looking at me with such high regard.
My girl, my world, my reason to live.
I look down at her knowing I have no choice but to keep going,
stay alive, live.

My husband, my best friend, my soulmate.
My one and only, putting up with me in such a state.
My hubby, my love, my reason to live.
So much he has done, given all he could give.

Family and friends, there till the end.
On them I came to depend.
So much support I received.
Having their support, I felt so relieved.
So lucky I feel.
My wonderful family and friends.

My reasons to live.

Aftermath

No one tells you what comes after...
The aftermath of cancer.

After the shock of a diagnosis,
After the talks about what is going to happen, the plan.
After a prognosis.
After the PET/CT scan.

No one tells you what comes after...
The aftermath of cancer.

After you've had infections.
After you've been to hospital numerous times.
After all the injections.
After picking yourself up and all the metaphorical climbs.

No one tells you what comes after...
The aftermath of cancer.

After the many, many treatments of chemo.
After all the waiting around.

After the many, many visits to Haemo.
After picking yourself up off the ground.

No one tells you what comes after...
The aftermath of cancer.

The trauma you may feel.
When it all suddenly feels real.
All the reflection.
Especially after that serious sepsis infection...

No one tells you what comes after...
The aftermath of cancer.

The muscle aches that don't go away.
The chemo fog that seems to stay.
How your brain wants to work in a different way.
How you don't always know what to say.

No one tells you what comes after...
The aftermath of cancer.

How you might view life completely differently.
Have a new perspective.
How life now seems quite simple, and you can absorb it
coherently.
How you're more reflective.

No one tells you what comes after...
The aftermath of cancer.

How much you value all the little things.
The things you used to take for granted at one time.
How you look forward to what life brings.
How proud you are of the mountain you've had to climb.

About the Author

Naomi lives in Cambridgeshire, originally from Lincolnshire. She lives with her wonderful husband, beautiful daughter, two crazy fur babies; Rocky and Blue and her chilled-out rabbit; Thumper.

Naomi is a qualified teacher and a Special Educational Needs Co-ordinator (SENCo). She works in a school for children with Social, Emotional and Mental Health (SEMH) difficulties. She has worked with both Primary and Secondary school age children.

Naomi began her career in teaching as a teaching assistant back in 2009. She then obtained a degree in 2017, and finally got her Qualified Teacher Status (QTS) in 2019.

Naomi became the school's SENCo and then took on the role of Designated Teacher. Essentially it is her responsibility to support the education of student's special educational needs and promote the educational needs of Looked After Children (LAC) within the school.

She has always been career driven, always set herself goals to aim for and been inspired by those around her to want to do well, make a difference and help others.

Naomi's family are incredibly important to her. She is one of three children and the oldest, having a younger brother and sister. She has always been close to her family, particularly her Mum, and her grandparents. When she married her husband

Robert, her family grew, and she gained in laws and a sister-in-law. She is pleased to say that they all get on extremely well and it is just like having another set of parents and another sister.

Let's see what else? She is a huge Disney fan! She loves it! She could not tell you about herself without mentioning it. Naomi has quite a few tattoos – including Disney ones...

Naomi likes to travel; her favourite place so far to visit has been Croatia. She enjoys swimming and walking the dogs as they are both good for mental health, it gives her time to think. She also loves reading and being able to escape into a good book. It is in part why she decided to start writing. Now she loves to read to her own daughter.

Naomi is planning to write more in the future.

You can connect with Naomi by visiting:
Facebook: @NaomiAndTheasBrilliantBookshop
Instagram: @naomi_n_theas_brill_bookshop